Understanding

Train of Thought

Lance Buck Paul Smith

authorHOUSE®

AuthorHouse™
1663 Liberty Drive, Suite 200
Bloomington, IN 47403
www.authorhouse.com
Phone: 1-800-839-8640

First published by AuthorHouse 9/7/2007

ISBN: 978-1-4343-2258-6 (sc)
ISBN: 978-1-4343-2259-3 (hc)

Library of Congress Control Number: 2007905310

Printed in the United States of America
Bloomington, Indiana

This book is printed on acid-free paper.

CONTENTS

Dedicated To My Parents

FOREWORD

This is a book about realization and a way of thinking. Many of the sayings, thoughts, and beliefs in this book have to do with etiquette, ethics, self-worth, and train of thought. Many of the analogies, anecdotes, and metaphors are just an insight into their meanings. This book contains outlooks that can be carried out and applied to many things in life. An incorrect train of thought can be like deadly poison. It can damage your mind and your spirit, and it can even be fatal.

Many of the short stories in this book are just a glimpse into a deeper meaning. The American Indians say that stories are like medicine; they have a lot of power.

Some of the sayings, thoughts, and beliefs in this book have been around for hundreds of years. Some come from ancient Japan and the way of the samurai. Some are very deep and it is hard to grasp their full or entire meaning. Some you should try to perceive in your own way, in a way that makes sense to you. One would think that the way of the samurai, a warrior's code from hundreds of years ago, would not apply in this day and age, but it does. It is not as much a way of life as it is a way of thinking.

Many of the sayings, thoughts, and beliefs in this book have come from my father, who was born in New York; a great man and a great father, without whom I would not be who I am. Many originate from the USA, some of which are just as profound as the ancient Japanese or samurai sayings, thoughts, and beliefs are. Some are common knowledge, which you may know and recognize, although they may be told from a different perspective.

The sayings, thoughts, and beliefs in this book cross my mind frequently in day-to-day circumstances; they have greatly affected my way of thinking. Understanding the contents of this book will produce an enhanced train of thought.

CHAPTER 1

Life and Death

Live Every Day Like It's Your Last

After all, how many more days will you have to live? Think about it. How many more sunrises will you get to watch? How many more walks in the park with your children or your friends will you get to have? Will you ever get another chance to walk on the beach with your lover? You never know when your time will come. If you knew this was your last day here on earth, what would you do, who would you go see, and what would you have done differently?

Seize The Day

Do not put off until tomorrow what you can do today. You might not be here tomorrow. You never know when the last time is that you will be able to do something. If you knew tomorrow was your last day to get something done—your last chance to get anything done—what would it be? What would you do? Carpe diem!

Life Is Short

Enjoy what you have while you have it. Time goes by fast, almost like a blur sometimes. It is evanescent, almost as if ten years goes by in what seems like one night's sleep. Take the time to enjoy that dance recital, take the time to go to see that school play. Enjoy it while it is here. It will all be over soon enough. When it is gone, you will miss it. This is one of life's hard lessons that everyone realizes in the end.

Love Every Day

Try to enjoy every day, whether it is good or bad. Although it may not be your last day, it may be your best day. Try to love each and every day. Today might be the greatest day you will ever know.

Realization

When someone has a near-death experience, they come to understand how short their time is and how near death they are. They value life more. They appreciate things more, especially the little things, like the sound of their lover's voice. They realize that each moment they are in, good or bad, is invaluable. They are aware that death is simply pending.

Live In The Moment

There is nothing more important than the present moment you are in. It is easy to spend your whole life thinking, worrying, or being concerned with what is going to happen, and life goes by so fast you think back about the things and the times that have passed. Sometimes it is hard to see or appreciate the moment that you are in. If you do not live in the moment you are in, then there will always be something on your mind or something bothering you.

Life is the single purpose of this immediate moment. If you can fully understand the value of the present moment, you will find that there is not much remorse about the past and not much concern about the future. Your past determines who and what you are. It is important not to forget it, and it is vital to prepare for the future. Nevertheless, there is nothing outside the immediate moment. Your entire life is nothing more than a secession of moments. Learn to live in each moment.

Understanding this train of thought is something that can be easy yet difficult to exact. You could spend a whole lifetime trying to master it.

Stop And Smell The Roses

Here is an old saying about enjoying, cherishing, understanding, and appreciating the moment you are in. It even applies to something as simple as work. You may be very frustrated with the mundane tasks at work, but your time here is very limited. Maybe you should take the time to look around you. Look at what is good about your work and what is good about the people you work with. Enjoy the time you are in and take the time to enjoy the moment. Cherish the moment.

Sign Of The Times

You should appreciate and enjoy the day and age you are in. You may reminisce about days gone by and how things used to be, but you must make the most out of the time you are in. There will come a day when others will think back and wonder about your day and age.

Although you could move back to a place where you once lived, the experiences would never be the same. It is good to remember the glory days, except you cannot live in them. Do not live in the past and do not live in the future. Live in the here and now.

Try Anything

You should try a lot of things in life. How else will you know whether or not they are for you? There may be something like escargot, for example, that may sound absolutely disgusting to you, but if you do not try it, how will you ever know whether or not you like it? Try it and you may find it to be the most succulent and luscious thing that you have ever tasted. Try new and different things. You never know.

Face Yourself

If you can live with yourself and with what you have done, then you can face yourself, and if you can face yourself, then you can face anyone. In the end, if you can face yourself, you can face anything.

Face-Off

Sometimes you get so caught up in the fights you fight every day that you lose sight of what it is you are fighting for. Every so often you should take a step back just to see the beauty in life so that you can remember why those fights are worth fighting.

Brass Balls

Like in the biblical story of David versus Goliath, sometimes you must face what seems to be the impossible, as if you are an ant facing off against an elephant. Even though you may get squished, you must have the courage to try your best to conquer the elephant. You must be willing to do whatever it takes. The valor lies in standing up, facing your opponent, and doing your best to strike him down.

Vengeance

Revenge is a dish best served cold. Time is on your side, but if you should decide to take revenge, go in headlong without hesitation. Victory is achieved in trying to accomplish, not in obtaining. Conversely, you should give justice a chance to prevail before exacting revenge.

Take It To The Grave

Some things are better off staying with you. If you are going to tell someone something that will hurt or may even destroy their life as they know it and it will not help another in any way, then perhaps you should not tell them. If it only helps you by getting it off of your chest and it is something that you caused in the first place, then you should have to suffer with it alone. Only a coward would hurt someone else just to make themselves feel better. Even if it is not something that you caused, if keeping it with you will keep another from suffering, then perhaps you should take it to the grave.

It's What You Do

It is what you do in life that counts. It does not have anything to do with what you look like, where you come from, or whom you are with. It is your actions that define you. In the end, it is what you do that matters.

Meditation

Meditating is significant to your mind and your spirit. One should meditate every day on being healthy, being strong mentally and physically, being happy, being successful, and on the inevitability of death. By meditating on death, you learn to overcome the fear of death. Death will happen; it is inescapable.

It's Better To Die Young

Be not afraid of death but of living too long. You may look at a very old person and think of how lucky that person is to have lived such a long life. On the contrary, that very old person has probably seen most of their loved ones buried and known unimaginable grief, turmoil, and pain. It might be that they are in a dreadfully lonely state of mind or are perhaps beginning to lose their mind. Conceivably, it is better to die young. Burying my children would be the hardest thing that I could ever do. I would rather my children bury me. The end is important in everything.

The Face Of Death

Laugh at the face of death. You should not fear it; death is as natural as being born. For hundreds if not thousands of years, great warriors such as the samurai meditated on the inevitability of death. Every day during peaceful times they would think of all the different ways of dying and consider themselves dead. This is not such a bad state of mind because no one knows when their time will come or how they will go, and life is too short to waste on fearing the end.

Laid To Rest

After your body is laid to rest, your spirit should continue on. Your beliefs and your knowledge should be taught so that they may be passed onto others. If you have done a good job raising your children and training your apprentices, then your spirit will live on through them. This is how you will be remembered and what you will be remembered for. In the end, it is all that will be passed on.

Memorialized

It is not when you were born and it is not when you die; it is what you have done in between your birth date and your death date that you will be recognized for. When you are talked about—whether it is about whom you were, what you were, or what your beliefs were—they will talk about everything you did during your time here. That timeline is what memorializes you.

Prepare For Death

When death strikes it can be swift, whether from an accident, an act of God, or a disease. It can come with little or no warning. Sometimes when death does come to you, it is as if the Grim Reaper himself has come to your door. It can leave you with very little or no time to prepare. Therefore, it is good to get your things in order before death comes knocking. Try not to leave too many burdens behind for your loved ones to deal with.

Remembrance

Gone but not forgotten. After you pass away, if you are buried at a gravesite, then your loved ones will have a place to mourn. When they can go to a tombstone and grieve, then they can leave some of that sadness there. When they are away from the gravesite, they can think of you without grieving as much. Contrarily, if your ashes are scattered, then your loved ones will not have a specific place to mourn, thus causing grieving to be almost synonymous with remembrance.

CHAPTER 2

Believing

Archenemy

You are your own worst enemy. When it comes down to it, you are the only one who can make you or break you. It is you and only you. It is in your own heart where you decide to make it or to give up. You control the inevitable, and only you decide your fate. Grab life by the horns and take it on headlong.

It is like running a twenty-mile marathon. If you are in good enough shape to run the first nineteen miles, then you are in good enough shape to run the last mile. However, your mind might tell you differently at mile nineteen. Your fate is what you make of it.

Inspiration

You have to find your motivation: something, anything that inspires you. There is a story about a man who crashed a small airplane while flying across the middle of the desert. He was middle-aged and not in top physical shape. He did not have any food or water, and the radio from the airplane was broken. It took ten days for search-and-rescue teams to find him. They said it was a miracle he survived. When he was asked what it was that kept him alive, he said, "I was going through a divorce and I did not want my soon-to-be ex-wife to get everything." The point is, whatever it is that inspires you, you need to find it.

Willpower

Where there is enough will, there is a mountain that can be moved. Having the will to survive is not good enough; you must also have the will to succeed. You are stronger than you know. With enough willpower you can change the world. If you believe in yourself and have the will to succeed, then you will be successful. If you do not believe in yourself, then no one else will ever believe in you. You have to have heart.

The most fundamental understanding of the way of the samurai is one's heart is the strongest weapon of all.

Endeavor

You must strive to be the best that you can be. It is not enough to go through life just doing well enough or accepting that things are just good enough. Always strive to do your best and to be your best. A good soldier dreams of becoming a general.

Pushing The Envelope

You never know how far you can go or even what you can do unless you try. How far can you ride a bicycle? You may only be able to ride it for five or ten miles, but after weeks and months of pushing the limit, you could possibly ride ten times that distance. The only way to know how far you can take something is to keep pushing your limit further and further. Or take something like golfing. You might take a swing for the first time and realize that you are a natural. The only way to find out if you are good at something is to try it.

You will never know what you are capable of until you try, and you will never know how far you can take something until you try. You always have to try.

The World Is At Your Fingertips

You can do anything you set your mind on doing. Try something you have never tried before and try your hardest. You might amaze yourself with what you can do. You must believe that anything is possible and have the will not to get discouraged.

Cowards never start, the weak give up along the way, but the strong see it through to the end.

Live Like A Lion, Not A Lamb

The best thing to do is the right thing. The next best thing to do is the wrong thing. The worst thing to do is nothing. Nothing ventured, nothing gained.

Destined For Greatness

It seems as though some people were just destined for certain things and some people never really figure out what their calling is. It may seem like a matter of fate, but it is not. You control your own destiny. Making your own way is what it is all about. If you want to write a book, just do it; write a book. If you want to start a business, just do it; start a business. Do not procrastinate; just do it. You get one life and one chance. So what if you fail. When it is all said and done, at least you will be able to say that you tried and you tried your best. When you are toward the end of your life, which do you think you will regret more: all the things you tried and failed or all the things you wish you would have tried but never did? Every great journey begins with a single step.

Only A Man

You are a man just like every other man who has ever stepped foot on this earth. Do not think that anything that another has achieved is unattainable; you are just like they are.

It all comes down to one man; every battalion, every company, and every country is controlled by a man. No matter what, when, or where, there is always just one man, a man just like you. You can attain anything that any other has achieved; you are inferior to no one.

Fortitude

There is nothing you cannot handle. To think that there is nothing that you cannot handle is not being conceited; it is being realistic. Think about it. Everything you have ever been faced with, no matter how good or how bad, you have faced and dealt with. If you look at things in this light, then you will know, no matter what faces you tomorrow, you can handle it.

Weather The Storm

What does not kill you makes you stronger. If it does not kill you, it will make you stronger because you will learn from it. The next time you have to deal with something like it, you will know how to handle it better. What does kill you may make someone else, who is close to you, stronger.

Eye Of The Storm

You could be basking in the sun one moment, then find yourself shipwrecked in the rocks the next. What makes you a man is what you do in the face of that storm.

Righteousness

Honorable men do not run away from their responsibilities; you must face up to your responsibilities no matter how tough they are. If you do not own up to and take care of your obligations, then you will not have any self-respect. Accordingly, if you do not have any honor and self-respect, then you will never be righteous.

Conviction

If to you something is right or has been done right, then it is right. Although others may disagree, that is their opinion. When you truly believe something is right or is done right, do not let others change your opinion, because to you it is what you believe it is.

It is sort of like President Thomas Jefferson once said: "In matters of style, swim with the currents, but in matters of principal, stand like a rock." Do not waver on what you believe.

Attitude Is Everything

A lot can be told from your attitude. Even if you have the ability to do something, if you do not believe wholeheartedly that you can do it, then your lack of confidence and spirit will show through in your attitude. No matter what it is, fifty percent of it is believing you can do it and fifty percent of it is doing it. You must be determined and believe you can achieve. That instills confidence and spirit, which invokes the right attitude.

A lot is relative to your attitude. People can sense a bad attitude, and the feeling will spread like toxicity. They can also sense and be inspired by a good attitude; hence the saying, "surround yourself with winners and you will be a winner." Attitude is extremely important.

Mover And Shaker

Having a reputation for getting it done or closing the deal is a good reputation to have. You must be powerful in order to be a dealmaker. Your power is projected through your confidence. If you are not confident the deal will go through, then the odds are the deal will not be done. You must believe in order to be confident.

Believing In Others

You can lead a horse to water, but you cannot make him drink. You can help guide others, but you can only hope they make the right choice; most people are who they are and they will do what they will do. You cannot force somebody to do something, to be something, or to make choices they do not want to make. You have to either accept people for what they are or let them go, but you cannot change someone's nature.

Dependent

You can depend on others, but if you depend too much on others, you could be let down often. Eventually you will have to depend on others for something, but you must always be ready to knuckle down and do it yourself.

Bridges

In the game of life, you will make friends and earn enemies; you will build bridges and from time to time you will burn bridges. Sometimes you will make enemies just by doing the right things. You cannot let what others may think or feel keep you from doing the right thing. May the bridges you burn light your way.

Dignity

As you go through life, you should always be proud to show your face. If you do something wrong, make up for it in some way to try and save face. Saving face is very important. Do not take it lightly. You should always be proud of what you do. Hold your head up and hold your head high. In doing so you will have dignity and you will earn the respect of others.

Be You

You have to be you in life. You are who you are, and you should never be ashamed of who you are. Do not conform to what others think, do not do something just because it is popular, and do not forsake something just because it is not popular. Be yourself. By doing so you will be at one with yourself. This is the basis of dignity.

Stand Tall

You should always take pride in yourself, your loved ones, your home, your country, and in everything that is yours. Even if you are not the tallest or your home is not the biggest and so on, always be proud of what you have and who you are. If you are not proud now, then you will never be proud.

Expectations

Sometimes it is hard to exceed expectations; however, if you try it is not hard to meet expectations. You do not necessarily need to do things better than you have done before, but you should always try to do things at least as good as you have done before.

Recompense

Never base your performance on what you are being paid or what your reward is. Always perform your very best and someday someone will recognize your worth and you will get what you deserve. Your reward will eventually equal your effort. This is the essence of work ethics.

Over And Above

You should always try to go beyond the call of duty, although when you do go that extra mile, some may say you do too much or they might critique your methods. Contrarily, when something goes wrong, everyone will say that you did not do enough or you did it the wrong way.

Right The First Time

As the old saying goes, anything worth doing is worth doing right. This is very true; many things have to be redone because they were not done right the first time. It takes more than twice as long and is more than twice as expensive to do something a second time around. If you take the extra time to do things right—to have the right materials, to have the right tools—then you can do things to the best of your ability. Always take pride in what you do and do everything the best that you can.

Enthuse

Do not set out halfheartedly. Believe in yourself and hit the ground running, just like a hawk that must be able to spot and fly quickly enough to catch a field mouse so he can eat or a field mouse that must not be the slowest field mouse that day or he will be caught and eaten by the hawk. Every day you must hit that ground running. It is essential for survival and success.

Determination

In ancient Japan it was believed that even if your head was to be cut off, you should be able to perform more actions. If you have great determination, your spirit should not die. What could be ascertained from this is that from the spirit of your convictions your men will show the same great determination that you did. Even if you, the master or leader, are killed, it will not stop your men from carrying out your will; nor will it change the ultimate outcome.

Never Give Up

The journey may be long and hard, and sometimes along the way you may get discouraged and lose heart, but do not give up. Look back at Abraham Lincoln and all the failures he had in his life. He started businesses that failed. He ran for Congress and lost. He ran for the Senate and lost. He ran for vice president and lost. Then he went on to become the president of the United States. He never gave up.

When it seems as though there is no hope, or when you are old and gray and you reach a point when something is or seems unobtainable or impossible, still you should never give up, because you never know. You have to believe.

CHAPTER 3

Feeling

Resolved

Say you are running late for work or for a meeting and you hurry as quickly as possible. Even by doing things like exceeding the speed limit and weaving in and out of traffic, you are still late and subsequently are all stressed out. Although you may be late, if you resolve yourself to being late from the start, then there will be no anxiety. This extends to everything. Be resolved from the beginning.

Peace Of Mind

To get something off of your mind, you must first resolve it in your mind. You should deliberate on things during times of peacefulness, such as in the evenings. Think it through thoroughly and try figuring out what the very best possible outcome would be and what the very worst possible outcome would be, and then try to figure out what the middle ground or halfway point for all involved would be. You can then put it out of your mind until the time comes to deal with it. When the time comes to settle it, it will probably settle close to what you have already established in your mind as fair.

Patience Is A Virtue

Good things come to those who wait. These old sayings have a lot of truth to them; however, they can be misconstrued as well. It is good not to make rash decisions and not to be in a rush. On the other hand, it is not good to put things off too long or you may run out of time before you have a chance to take care of them. There is no time like the present. Practice patience, not procrastination.

A Child

There is nothing as great or as pure as the love of a child. It is one that I would truly give my life for. If my child was dying and needed a new heart in order to survive and there were no donors, or the list was so long that we would run out of time, then without hesitation I would take my life so that my child could have mine.

Honestly how many other things in life are your convictions that strong for? This sort of love, this feeling, is truly something that everyone should experience at least once in their life.

Never Say Never

Although it is easy to say you would never and to honestly feel you would never, times change and people change. Everything keeps changing. As you grow older, you grow wiser and your feelings change. You realize how short life is and how few new experiences there are.

Where You Are

Life is about the journey, not the reward. It is not so much where you are going or where you came from; it is more where you are at right now. The journey is what you must learn to savor. If you are not happy along the way, then you will not be happy when you get to where it is that you are going.

It is not how much money you make, what kind of car you drive, or the house you live in. It is rather the people you meet and the relationships that you have along the way.

Man's Best Friend

A lot can be learned from a dog. When a dog is hungry, he eats. When he is thirsty, he drinks. When he is tired, he sleeps, yet in an instant he is up and ready to go. He loves receiving affection from his master, being rubbed and petted. He is never embarrassed or ashamed of his actions, good or bad. His primal instinct is pure and natural. Perhaps it is because the dog's nature is so straightforward and honest that man admires him very much.

Form Is Emptiness Is Form

Form is emptiness. In sword-fighting, if you do not have a style or a rhythm, then your opponent will not be able to interrupt it. Not having a style is a style in itself. This is your form as emptiness.

Emptiness is form. Sometimes you do things a certain way just because it feels natural to you. This is emptiness as form.

Sixth Sense

Many believe there is a sixth sense. The five senses are seeing, hearing, smelling, tasting, and touching. The sixth is being able to sense something or to mentally feel its presence.

In my youth, while in martial arts, we would practice sitting with our eyes closed meditating, trying to sense when one of the instructors would strike one of us with a soft plastic throwing star. In my experiences this sixth sense does seem to work. It is not exact, but it does work. Meditation helps you obtain it.

Premonitions

Now and then you can just feel things. Sometimes you feel it in your gut and you know something is just not right. If you get the feeling something is wrong with a deal you are going to make, with someone you are going to do a deal with, or even with someone you are going to hire, then do not go through with it. Trust your instincts.

Walk A Mile

You should not be too quick to judge. You never know what someone has been through. They could have suffered unimaginable losses and unspeakable horrors. When you see someone down on their luck, you do not need to show them compassion, but do not disrespect them either. As the old saying goes, do not judge a man until you have walked a mile in his shoes. Every man deserves a chance.

Fool Me Once

Fool me once, shame on you. Fool me twice, shame on me. Fool me a third time, and I am just a fool.

You give someone a chance and they let you down. Shame on them for letting you down. You give them a second chance and they let you down. Shame on you for giving them a second chance. After all, they had already proven to you that they were not worthy. If you give them a third chance and they let you down, well, you are just a fool.

As the old saying goes, once bitten, twice shy. Once you have been bitten or burned, you should be leery of giving someone a second chance.

Birds Of A Feather

It is a wonder how an eagle knows it is an eagle or how a vulture knows it is a vulture. They just instinctively know. This is true for all walks of life. For instance, you can tell a lot about a person by looking at their friends. Whether at work, school, or even prison, similar people seem to find and respond well to each other. Whether someone is good or bad can be discerned through their friends. Birds of a feather do flock together.

Human Nature

Whether it is family, friends, or acquaintances, eventually their true colors will shine through. Some people will take advantage of their friends and relatives. At times they may try to straighten up by sobering up or making promises, and it may seem like they do not take advantage of the situation as much, but sometimes they do and they never stop. If someone is related to you or very close to you, although they should get more chances, it does not mean they should get endless chances. If a friend or relative never stops hurting you, then eventually you need to cut the ties or stop the bleeding. Some people never change; it is their nature.

There is an old story about a frog and a scorpion. The frog and the scorpion lived on different parts of an island in the middle of a large lake. One day there was a great storm and soon the lake started to rise. The island began to flood and eventually it shrunk to almost nothing. Then as the frog was about to swim to safety, the scorpion asked if he could please get a ride over to the other side of the lake. The frog said, "If I give you a ride on my back, how do I know you will not sting me?" The scorpion replied, "If I sting you, you will die and sink to the bottom of the lake. If I do that while I am on your back, I will drown. Do you honestly think that I would do that?" So the frog thought about it awhile, and then he agreed to give the scorpion a ride. Halfway across the lake the scorpion sunk his stinger into the frog's back and the frog said, "Why did you do that? Now we will both die." The scorpion replied, "I could not help it. I am a scorpion. That is my nature."

Never Forget

Having a long memory is good. You do not necessarily need to remember all of the details about someone or something. Just remembering the fact that the experience was good or bad is enough. Memories are like scars. Although they may fade away over time, they will always be a part of you.

Distance

Hatred is a bad thing. It is okay not to like someone or not to care about someone, but do not let it consume you. Disown them if need be or have nothing to do with them, but do not harbor resentment. Distance yourself and learn to let it go.

Do The Right Thing

To know if you are honestly doing the right thing, all you need to do is ask yourself, and in your heart is where you will find the answer.

Do Onto Others

Do onto others as you would have them do onto you. Even though this is a biblical saying, it is a saying that is used a lot. I think some part of it is correct, as in "show respect to others so others will show respect to you," although to look at it from a different perspective, to give all your hard-earned money to someone else or some organization and expect that someone else or some organization will take care of you would be unwise. You should treat others right, but do not be foolish and expect anything in return.

Undertaking

Do not only think of telling your workers what to do; also do things yourself so that you may know what they are like. This will enable you to know what you are asking of your workers and what to expect out of them. Do not hesitate to get your hands dirty.

It's A Dirty Job

Being the boss can be a dirty job, and it is one of the harder jobs there is. Giving bad news to employees, such as "work is slow" or "you are being replaced," is not easy. Having to let someone go, especially right before the holidays, can be a very difficult task. Nevertheless, every job needs to be done whether it is firing people, flipping burgers, or cleaning toilets. Somebody has to do it. If you do not do it, then someone else will. No matter what your job is, you should do it diligently and never let doing your job have a negative effect on you.

Nice Guys Finish Last

If you are too nice to people, they may try to take advantage of you. They might mistake your niceness for weakness. You should not appear too nice, yet you do not need to be mean. If you are unpleasant enough, people will think twice before they try to take advantage of you. Balance is important to everything.

It's Just Business

Take your work seriously, not personally; leave your emotions at the door. If you lose a job or a deal falls through, do not let it affect you the way losing a loved one would affect you. You need to take it seriously, but it is only business. It is not that you will be unscathed by the consequences; it is that you cannot let it affect you on a personal level. When dealing with business, it is all about business and nothing else. When you do this, some may view you as cold or callous, but it is not about feelings; it is about business.

When you can put your emotions to the wayside, you can free up or open up your mind so that you can think about the business at hand. This is the basis of a shrewd businessman.

Working And Living

When working for a living, your motivation is survival. You cannot afford to lose your job, you need to put food on the table, and you live paycheck to paycheck. Something can be said about a worker like this. You are more apt to show up on time, work hard, and so on.

Living for working, on the other hand, takes a totally different type of motivation. It is completely the opposite. You are not totally dependent on a paycheck and you can risk losing your job. It takes passion and endurance to keep working when you do not have to. Your motivation might be that you need a pastime or that you love your work.

You may start out in life with that instinctive survival motivation, though when you get to the point when you no longer need to work for a living, it takes a special inspiration to work, one that comes from the heart.

In Your Blood

For someone who was born on a farm, as far back as they can remember, they have been farming. Someone who's father was a baker as a child might have gone to his father's bakery and helped him bake. If you are born into something, then you will probably be very good at it because you will have practiced it since a young age.

Sometimes people never focus on one thing. They may figure it is good to know a little something about a lot of different things. Being a jack of all trades is good, but to be really good at one thing is significant. If you never dedicate yourself to a certain thing or a particular area, then you will probably never be very good at any one thing.

You should do what comes naturally. That is what is in your blood. Whether you are born into something or not, if you do what comes naturally to you and you specialize in a specific area, you will excel. To find your calling in life, just do what comes naturally.

A Born Leader

A leader must be willing to do whatever it takes. If you are not willing to go all the way, then you will not have the respect of your crew, and subsequently they may not follow you in all the way.

There are military tactics on leadership that have been used for hundreds of years. For instance, the leader in the US cavalry from the 1700s and 1800s would literally lead his troops into battle. If the troops saw he was willing to risk it all, then they would risk it all by trying to impress and protect him.

Moreover, there are the modern-day Navy Seals; the troop leader goes into battle with his men. He does not dine or sleep in the officers' quarters; he dines and sleeps with his men. A Navy Seal team is four to six men with the leader being one of them. They go behind enemy lines and they depend solely upon each other. They feel equal in this situation, yet one is the leader. He has the respect of his men both as a colleague and as a leader.

The key is not to put yourself above them. You are both men; you are both equals. It just so happens that you are the leader as well. You must always be willing to go in headlong. By doing so you will have the respect and admiration of your troops.

Laying It On The Line

It is said you must go outside of your comfort zone in order to be successful. You definitely need to take chances; however, if you live in the moment you will not necessarily be outside of your comfort zone.

– is not needed.

Win Or Lose

Everybody wants to win and somebody has to lose. If you are not in it to win it, then you should get out of the game. Of course you should want to win. That is instinctive. Wanting to win may come naturally, but having heart does not. What defines a winner is not whether you want to win but how much effort you put into trying to win. The heart of a person determines whether or not he is a winner.

It is not a matter of accomplishing the goal as much as it is a matter of trying your best to achieve the goal; the honor and the pride lie in trying your best. If you show courage and go in headlong, giving every ounce of your body and soul, then you have what it takes. That is where the victory is gained. It truly is not a matter of whether you win or lose.

It is like if you played against a great team and they barely won because time ran out, or because they had the advantage, like the wind to their backs or the sun in your eyes. Are there more honors for the people who were on the sidelines the whole time for the winning team, or are there more honors for the defeated players who have played their hearts out? It is the latter.

Persevere

If you start something, you should finish it. Completing things is very important; it instills self-confidence. When you have completed something, you can step back and take pride in what you have created. It gives you a sense of accomplishment. You should always try to see things through to the end.

Confront Your Demons

You alone must stand up to your fears and be prepared to fight any and every battle that confronts you. It is in your best interest to go it alone. If you fail then you will have no one to blame but yourself. The less people you have to blame, the more you will learn to depend on yourself.

Trepidation

The oldest and strongest kind of fear is fear of the unknown. Fear itself is concern and excitement about what might happen in the next moment. By living in the immediate moment, you have a tremendous amount of control over your feelings. Fear is nothing more than a momentary feeling, which can be dismissed as quickly as it was found. You should not be apprehensive about a moment that you are not yet in.

Fear No Man

Everything that has ever been done to you has been done to you by another man. Every deal that is overthrown is done by the means of another man. Every person who is murdered is murdered as the result of another man's actions. Fearing no man is the wrong philosophy. You should fear nothing; nonetheless, you should be extremely cautious of man.

There Is Nothing To Fear

As a child I was scared of the dark water in the shadowy part of the lake. My father would say, "What is there to be scared of? Think about it. There are no sharks or alligators in the lake." He was right. I would face my fears and dive into the water. I continued to use this metaphor throughout different parts of my life.

You Only Live Once

If you want to try something, you should try it no matter what your fears are. For instance, are you afraid you might die in an accident if you try something like skydiving or bungee jumping? What if you do die trying it? Is it better to sit on the sidelines all your life thinking about what it must be like? You should not fear anything. Definitely do not fear death. There is nothing you can do to stop it. Accept it and resolve your feelings about it.

Scared To Death

In my late teens, I apprenticed in a trade that required me to work at great heights. Of course with this came the fear of falling. If you do not get over the fear of falling, the anxiety can be overwhelming. It can keep you from focusing, which can cost you your life. So I would think, *What are you afraid of? The worst possible thing that could happen is you could be killed.* By accepting the fact that I could die, it was as if I had arrived. If you learn not to fear death, then there is nothing to fear.

A Fate Worse Than Death

Worrying can be a fate worse than death. Worrying about something can cause a great deal of turmoil; it can cause pain and suffering, insomnia, and even serious medical conditions like ulcers and nervous breakdowns. You cannot let worrying about the outcome of something overpower you; let the chips fall where they may. A good outlook is just like that old saying, "Whatever will be, will be." It is not that you do not care what the outcome will be. It is that you are not going to let what might be the outcome consume you.

When you think about it, someone on death row worrying about being put to death for ten or more years may very well have suffered a fate worse than death.

CHAPTER 4

Seeing

Dream State

When something terrible is happening to you, you can look at it as if it is only a dream. If you wind up in something atrocious, like a horrific accident, or in the middle of a battlefield, the reality can be brutal and absolutely devastating. It could throw you into a state of shock and paralyze you. In these sorts of times, think of it as a bad dream, just like after awakening from a nightmare you think to yourself, *It was just a dream.* By putting your mind into this dream state, even if just for a few minutes, you can deal with an unthinkable situation. Having this viewpoint can make devastating times and events more bearable, even if just for the moment.

Whatever the scenario, whatever the case may be, soon it will only be in your dreams.

The Mind's Eye

When looking into the mirror at age fifty, you see an older man looking back at you, yet when you are not looking in the mirror, your mind's eye still sees you as that strong young man that you used to be. This is being young at heart as your body grows older and shows signs of age. Do not doubt your eyes' perception, but learn to take pleasure in the view from your mind's eye.

Emergence

Although you should not judge a book by its cover or a man by his appearance, a lot of people do. Appearance is very important. Whether you are a white-collar worker or a blue-collar worker, you must look respectable. It may happen on occasion, when you are under the weather or not getting enough sleep, that your appearance may be poor. Even in such times, it is good to try to make yourself appear as suitable as possible. Image is important.

Furthermore, people can read a lot about you by the small details, as in how your desk or garage is kept or how your hair and nails are kept. If you are not well groomed and your desk or garage is in disarray, then your life and business might be in disarray as well. Appearance is significant.

Mentor

It is always good to have someone to look up to or aspire to. And you should keep in mind that through life, as you may be looking up to someone else, someone else may be looking up to you. A mentor is essential.

Pocketknife

No one ever plans on being stranded, but it does happen. No one ever plans on being attacked and having to defend themselves, but this also happens. Something as simple as a pocketknife can help save your life. You should always carry one.

Expect The Unexpected

When you pull up to a stoplight or a stop sign, expect that someone could ram into you or carjack you. You should always check your mirrors and keep your doors locked. Leave space between you and the car in front of you so you can pull away quickly if needed. When you go out to your car in the morning or when you return home in the evening or from vacation, there could be someone waiting to confront you or kill you. You could startle someone in the middle of something, which might make them act out of fear of being caught. Be ready for and expect misfortune, confrontation, battle—anything and everything.

Even during a walk in the park or during the day at the office, there could be an incident you did not expect. Always be aware of your surroundings. Expecting the unexpected should be applied to every aspect of life.

Affliction

It is good to save for a rainy day. Perhaps a loved one needs some help and they must lean on you, or you could fall ill or lose your job. Thus when times are good you should always put a little bit aside. If you prepare for adversity, you will be able to overcome it. As sure as there are good times, there will be bad times. Prepare for the future. You never know what will ensue.

Adapt And Overcome

Go through or go around; go over or go under. Do whatever it takes to achieve. Adapt to every problem that you are faced with and view everything in your way as an obstacle that you can overcome. This is a great point of view to have: to do whatever it takes and to not let anything stop you. Where there is a will, there is a way.

Less Is More

If you have a hundred pictures on the wall but only a few are great and the rest are just good, then it is harder to appreciate the few great ones when they are camouflaged by all the others. Or another scenario is if you have so many things in your garage that when the time comes to try to find something you cannot and you end up buying a new one, then several months later you run across it and now you own two. Less is more in many ways.

Organize

Organization is very important. When something important comes up and you cannot find what you need, it is very hard to perform well. If you keep organized, especially all the small things like the paperwork in your files or the tools in your toolbox, then you will be capable of performing better. If you are not organized, then your ability will be lessened.

Study

Learning is endless; always keep your mind open. Studying something is like a never-ending journey. If you think that you have learned everything there is to know about something, then you have just closed your mind and limited your possibilities. You will never learn everything there is to know about anything. Does anyone ever truly master anything?

Time Is Of The Essence

Make the most of your time. If you are going to study, then study; if you do not want to study, then do not. Be in accord with one or the other, but do not mix the two. It is bad when one thing becomes two. You should keep things separate whenever possible. This applies to everything in life.

Matter Of Time

You should not look at things as a matter of time. There are twenty-four hours in the day. You can find the time. If you do not look at things as a matter of time, then you will be able to focus better on the tasks at hand. It is not a matter of time; you have all your time in this world.

It is like what Benjamin Franklin once said, "A man that sleeps more than three hours a night is just pure lazy." Obviously that lack of sleep would lead to an unclear mind. I believe what he was saying is that there is enough time in the day to do what you need to do, even if it takes only getting three hours of sleep.

In The Fast Lane

If you run an engine or your body at full throttle continuously, then it will break down fast and it will not last. If you expect your vehicle or body to last, then you must take care of it. It is okay to run hard some of the time but not all of the time. Self-discipline should be practiced.

Running On Empty

You can run your crews ten hours a day, six days a week, but if you do so, production will decrease. There is a limit to what you can effectively get out of a crew. Weekends, holidays, and vacations are vital to the mind and spirit. People must rest. It is crucial.

Mistakes

You should try to learn from your mistakes and from the mistakes of others. Quite often several different people make the same mistake over a long period of time. This is usually due to the fact that no one is paying attention to the mistakes that others have made. Learn from your mistakes, learn from the mistakes of others, and you can learn from the mistakes that are not made as well.

Accountability

You have to be accountable. Always accept responsibility for your actions, whether the consequences are good or bad. If you are the boss, foreman, or manager, always accept responsibility for the actions of your group. If the worker or workers under you do something wrong, do not let the blame ride on them. You are the supervisor. It is your responsibility. You must be accountable for the good and the bad. It is just as important to take the credit as it is to take the blame. By doing so you will gain the respect and admiration of others. This is the basis of nobility.

Pay Attention

When you are at work, focus on work. When you do not, that is when mistakes happen. Depending on your line of work, it could cost you or one of your coworkers his life. Always pay attention to the task at hand. Do not think about last weekend or the party coming up next weekend. The minute you take your mind off of your work is the split second a life-altering mistake can happen.

You should always pay attention, even to something as simple as watching where you step. You never know what you might be ready to step on, over, or in front of. You could be ready to step onto a rusty nail, you could be ready to step over a one-hundred-dollar bill, or you could be ready to step in front of an oncoming truck. Watch your step and pay attention to everything.

Stay Focused

When you set your eyes on something, do not waver from it. Even though you may see something else, do not lose your concentration. Do not give your attention to anything other than the one that you have first set your eyes on.

Sometimes you may be distracted, which makes it hard to concentrate and stay focused, but you should always try to obtain what it is you first focused on.

Probability

If it looks like it, then it probably is it. If it looks like chocolate, smells like chocolate, and tastes like chocolate, then it probably is chocolate. But it may not be chocolate. Always be cautious. Just because something may look like, smell like, and taste like something in particular does not mean that it is.

Moreover, if you hear of something that sounds too good to be true, then it probably is.

Superficial

Beauty is only skin deep. Someone or something that is attractive or beautiful on the outside could be ugly on the inside. You should learn to look at more than just the façade. Look at the bigger picture and try to see all that there is to see. True beauty is felt through the heart, not seen through the eyes.

Vanity

If you have the absolute prettiest person, car, home, or anything like that as yours, you will notice that a lot of people will want to take it away from you. On the other hand, even if the one that you have is not the prettiest or the finest, there may still be a few who would like to take it away from you.

In The Eye Of The Beholder

As if with a painting, how can anybody but the artist say, when the final brushstroke is made, when it is beautiful, when it is finished?

Look at a priceless painting from a hundred years or more ago. It was only up to the one who created it to say that it was complete and that it was beautiful. When it was first completed, there may very well have been those who critiqued the painting. However, many years later, after all the critics are dead and buried, all that remains is a priceless painting that many clearly agree is beautiful.

If you create something and to you it is complete and beautiful, then that is what it is. Just because others may not be able to see the beauty in it now does not mean that it does not exist.

One Man's Treasure

One man's trash is another man's treasure. Someone may not be able to see the value in something and someone else might be able to. You should keep in mind that just because nobody else sees any value in an idea or a concept that you have, or in something that you have created, does not mean that it is not worth a fortune. Believe in your dreams.

As Good As It Gets

The grass does not get any greener on the other side of the hill. Say you move to a house on the other side of town or in the next town because it has a lush green lawn and a nice paintjob. If you have the same habits and give the new house the same upkeep, then things will end up just like they were at your old house. You should take care of what you have. This pertains to much more than just the material things in life.

Make The Most Of It

When life hands you lemons, make lemonade. This is a good outlook to have: to try and make the most out of things. Someone might look at a backyard that has nothing planted and think that it is nothing but a bunch of dirt. Another might look at that same backyard and think that it has rich soil and the beginnings of a beautiful garden. You should always try to see something in everything.

Take Horatio Nelson for example, a great British naval leader from the 1700s. The first battleship he was given was not the prize of the fleet. It was one of the smallest, oldest, and weakest ships, and almost every adversary he faced outgunned him. He had twenty cannons on his ship and he would go up against ships that had sixty cannons. He developed tactics that gave him an advantage. He learned how to out maneuver the large ships with his smaller ship. He could get set and fire his twenty cannons and then maneuver his smaller ship around fast enough to where he could reload, get set, and fire another twenty cannons before the larger ship could ever get set and fire its cannons. He would continue this onslaught until he defeated the enemy. He learned to dominate the sea with less of a battleship than almost everyone he faced. He looked for and was able to see the value in something, whereas others could not see any.

This tactic is studied and used by military leaders to this day. It is known as the Nelson tactic. This does not mean that you should bring a knife to a gunfight. However, if all you have is a knife and you find yourself in a gunfight, then try to see what you can do with the knife, not what the knife can do for you.

Two Good Eyes

Sometimes it is as though you have two good eyes, yet you are still not able to see. You should try to see everything around you, but always try to focus on each specific point. At times you may have to back up or distance yourself in order to see things from a different angle or a different light. On occasion it is good to have a second set of eyes look at it with you. Sometimes it is difficult to see what has been right in front of you the whole time.

A Picture Is Worth

A lot can be learned by watching someone do something. Sometimes it is better to not ask questions and just to observe. If a picture is worth a thousand words, then watching something in real life is worth ten thousand words.

Your Opponent's Method

It is good to study other styles, systems, and methods. Although you may have a superior method, times change and methods improve. When you can see your opponent's method, then you can see how to disrupt it or how to supersede it. This extends to many things.

Winds Of Change

You should always be prepared for something to change. Eventually everything will. You should try to anticipate, adjust for, and adapt to changes. If you can foresee an upcoming change, you might be able to gain an advantage. Whether it is for the good or the bad, everything will change.

Change The Things You Can

Some things you can change and some things you cannot. You should learn to recognize things in this way. Accept that there are things that you cannot change. Like a train wreck, you may see it coming, but there is nothing you can do to stop it. If it is something that you cannot change, then do not waste your energy trying to change it. If it is something that you can change, then you should do your best to change it.

Find Your Center

Effectiveness of motion: it is kind of like that carnival game with the big sledgehammer and the thirty-foot pole, with a target at the bottom and a bell at the top. You can see a great big, strong man hit the target as hard as he can, time and time again swinging the hammer with a tremendous amount of force and strength, but the slide does not reach the top. Then a small, meek man comes along and with one swift, fluid swing of the hammer, the slide shoots to the top and rings the bell. It is not how hard you hit the target; it is how precisely you strike the target. Your efforts have to be concentrated. One could extend this understanding to many things.

It's Not What You've Got

Who is more valuable? Someone who is doing the best they can and producing eight pieces per day or someone who has the ability and skill to produce ten pieces per day but is only producing eight pieces per day? Production wise, they are the same; ability wise, one is more skilled but will not use his skills. Performance wise, the one who is less skilled performs at his peak. He gives you all he has to give, which is admirable.

It is not a matter of what you have to give as much as it is a matter of what you give. If someone gives you all they have to give, then that is all you can ask for. Even if they are not the best or biggest producer, if they are doing their best and producing as much as they can, then that is commendable.

Employee Standards

The three most important qualities in an employee are production, dependability, and loyalty. If you take away any one of these three traits, then the employee is not worth keeping.

Sometimes an employee will have these three qualities and work years on end without fail. Then for some reason, perhaps problems in their personal life, they stop caring and it becomes apparent in the quality of their work. If this is an employee who has been a good producer, dependable, and loyal, then you should also show your loyalty and give him a chance to recover. Eventually he will have to care about his work again, but if he does not, then you have to let him go.

Employees' Worth

An employee's worth can be based on their replacement value. Even if they are very good, you can still base their worth on what it would cost you to hire someone else in their place.

Equality

No matter the task, no matter the duty; no one man's job is more important than another one's. There is no difference in honor or dignity between one person and the next, provided that he fulfills his task or duty to the best of his ability.

The Way It Is

On occasion you may hope that something will turn out a certain way or wish that something would have turned out differently. Nevertheless, you need to accept things the way they are. In the end, it is what it is.

CHAPTER 5

Thinking

Attention To Details

The little things are very important. If you make sure all the little things are taken care of, then usually the bigger things will work out well. At times it may appear that you have no control over something; however, by paying attention to the smaller things, you may have an effect on the uncontrollable.

This could happen if you are raising your children and doing your best as a parent to teach them what is right. You are making sure they do their homework, get plenty of rest, eat right, and take care of themselves. When the time comes for them to take an important test, from your teachings and your discipline they will probably do well. Even if they do not, you cannot take the test for them. You did all the little things, which was all that you could do.

You have a tremendous amount of power over the small details. No matter the size of the goal or task, if you pay attention to and take care of the details, then you should be able to accomplish it successfully.

Even In War

Even in war, if you have all your ducks in a row, or you are prepared by having all of the small things in order, this will enable you to win the smaller battles. In winning the smaller battles, you will ultimately win the war. Pay attention to the little things.

Preparedness

Life will have many crossroads—crossroads of opportunity and readiness. You should be prepared when an opportunity presents itself. How many times have you passed up an opportunity or a good deal because you were not prepared to act on it? Be ready for opportunity.

Master Plan

Although you may have an idea of what you need to do in a week, a month, or even longer down the road, it is hard to plan the exact details that far in advance. Of course, you should have a master plan or a long-term plan, but in order to achieve it, you must simply plan the specific details for the upcoming day and try to carry them out. To have a plan of attack for tomorrow is essential.

Priorities

Make a list of all your goals and then prioritize them. If you take care of one item on your list at a time, regardless if it takes one day or one year per item, eventually you will accomplish everything on your list. Keeping on top of things is nothing more than taking care of your priorities one small detail at a time.

Closure

You should always try to finish what you start; otherwise it will remain incomplete in your mind. Even if something is not turning out quite right or quite the way you had hoped, you should still finish it. Putting an end to things or putting them to bed is important in unfettering the mind.

Being Successful

The difference between being successful and not is the decisions you make in life. Whether you think it is a minor decision or a major decision, all decisions have an effect on your life, such as what to eat or how much to eat, whether you should exercise or how much you should exercise, where to go to school or how long to stay in school, what job to take or whether to relocate to take a job, and whether you should rent a house or buy a house and where to buy a house. Where you are right now was determined by the decisions that you have made.

The decisions you make in life are all that separate you from being rich or poor. You could find one of the richest men in the world with the same upbringing and beginnings as some bum on the street, and the main difference between them is the decisions they have made in life.

It's Your Decision

Open-mindedness is a virtue. You should listen to the advice of others and take it into consideration. Like the old saying goes, two minds are better than one. Though ultimately, if it is your decision to make, then you must make it. Do not let others make your decisions for you.

Calm, Cool, And Collected

When confronted with making a difficult decision on something that is very serious and very important, even if you think you know what the right decision would be, you should not decide on it right away. You should think it through thoroughly during times of normalcy and resolve yourself to the fact that your decision may have great consequences. Once you have settled it in your mind, then you can come back with a lucid decision.

Heat Of The Moment

Try not to decide something in the heat of the moment. Sometimes you must make decisions in stressful situations, but whenever possible, take a break or call them right back. Try to take a moment to think it through. Under stress it is harder to make a good decision. This is not being indecisive; it is a matter of not being pressured into a decision.

Grace Under Fire

In extreme situations, when you are forced to make decisions under pressure, the key is to stay calm and settled down. By doing so you can think clearer and make better decisions. Of course, to stay calm and settled under extreme conditions is a difficult thing to do. The way to do it is to not concern yourself with what the consequences of your decisions might be. Certainly you care what the consequences will be, and that must weigh into your decision, but you have to look at it as if you are deciding it for someone else. It is like a lawyer deciding what statements or arguments to make. It could be the difference of whether someone lives or dies, yet he can think clearly because it is not his life that hangs in the balance. Even when things seem overwhelming, stay calm and focused. Eventually you will have things under control.

Decisiveness

In life you must make decisions. Be decisive. It is very important. Hopefully you will make more good decisions than bad decisions, but ultimately it is better to have made a bad or poor decision than to have not made a decision at all. When you have made a decision, do not second-guess yourself. If you do there could be no end to it. Just make the best decision you can and then stick with it. If it was a bad decision, then you can learn from it.

In ancient Japan they believed you should have great spirit and determination, and when you need to, you should be able to decide in an instant.

Integrity

In life you will inevitably make some bad decisions. What defines you is how you deal with them. When you make a bad decision, pull yourself up by the bootstraps, dust yourself off, get your mind right, and deal with it. Always try to make the best decisions you can, but regardless, you must accept the consequences for the decisions you have made and deal with them responsibly.

Getting Away With It

Sometimes you do get away with something big; like the old saying goes, getting away with murder. Conversely, if you go through life figuring that you will not get away with anything, then chances are you will make different or better decisions. No one should get away with murder, and hardly anyone ever does.

Appease

Being the boss is a tough row to hoe, and quite often you need to make
hard decisions, which are expected to be good ones. No matter how hard
you try, you cannot keep everyone happy, and no matter what you do,
eventually someone will grow unhappy. All you can do is try to keep all
of your workers and people as comfortable as possible with the decisions
you make.

Necessary Evil

It is a dog-eat-dog world out there. Still you must try to do the right thing. You have to do what you have to do. When you do so, this sometimes upsets people and relationships. If it is something that must be done, then you must do it regardless of the consequences or what others may think. Just because others may view you as ruthless or a tyrant does not mean that it is true. They may not be able to see the whole picture or know the full story.

Principles

Never lower your standards to another's, especially in business or in battle. Always do what is right. Just because you are going up against someone whose morals or values are low does not mean you should lower yourself to their level. Try to stay above it or rise above it. In the end, by transcending, win or lose, you will still have your dignity.

Get It Right

Get your mind right. You must settle things in your mind before dealing with others. If you do not have it right in your own mind first, then you will never be able to settle it with anyone else.

Mindset

You must have the right frame of mind. Even if you just exist in society, when your mindset is too far off, you will be locked up or condemned. You must conform enough to be accepted by common laws, but this does not mean you have to do everything that you are told. You must be levelheaded but you should also be strong-minded.

The Mind Is A Weapon

The mind is a powerful weapon and the best one that you could ever have. Every battle is won and every enemy is defeated with this weapon. Many times in life this will be the only weapon that you have at your disposal. Never forget or misjudge this weapon. Its potential is endless. Learn to harness some of its power.

Mind Over Matter

If you do not mind, then it does not matter. Still you can let others believe that something has affected you when it has not. This way they think they have accomplished what they had set out to do, but if it truly does not bother you, then it does not matter. There is a way of controlling a situation when it appears that you have no control over it at all. This is one way of applying the mind's power over a matter.

The Best Laid Plans

The best way to execute a plan is to take care of all the little things; all the fine details. But if a plan does not work, it usually falls apart little by little. You must be able to deal with each part of the plan that falls apart as it arises. It is not so much a matter of having a backup plan per say as it is being able to roll with the punches. If you stay calm and make the best decisions you can on each problem that presents itself, then usually everything will work out as well as can be expected. More often than not, the backup plan is simply to modify the original plan.

Chose Your Battles

If you fight every battle as hard as you can, regardless of whether you can win or not, then you take your energy away from the battles that you have a chance of winning. Do not put as much time and energy toward battles that are not winnable. Concentrate and focus your efforts on the battles that you can win.

It is not a matter of whether you are right or wrong as much as it is a matter of whether you can win or not. Just because you know when to throw in the towel does not mean that you are weak or you are a pushover. Choose your battles carefully. You cannot win them all.

Get In The Game

Learning the basics about something is important. Take baseball for example. You need to practice all the fundamentals, like throwing, catching, and hitting the ball, but when it is game time, you need to know where to make the play. You could be the best at throwing, catching, and hitting, but in the heat of the moment, if you do not know where the play is or where to throw the ball, then you will not be a proficient ballplayer. The basics are important, but so is strategy. They should both be studied and practiced; they should both become second nature. This applies to many things.

Never Underestimate

Never underestimate anyone. You should always assume your opponent is more skilled than you and that they know everything about you. This is one of the most significant things when dealing with anyone in life. Whether it is in business with competitors, in a game with friends, or even in war with enemies, you should always assume that they know more or can do more than they are letting be known.

What You Don't Know

Sometimes people say what you do not know will not hurt you, but this is not true. If others are conspiring against you and you do not know it, then this is something that you do not know and it will hurt you. Everything you do not know about your opponent can hurt you. You should never think that something you do not know would not hurt you.

You should always keep in mind that, although you may not know what your opponent's weaknesses are, you surely know what yours are.

Keep Your Enemy

Keep your friends close and your enemies closer. The more you know about your enemy, the better you can defend, react, or conquer. On the same token, you should try not to show your side, or if you must, then try to show a side you would rather they see.

Hope For The Best

Hope for the best but prepare for the worst. This is an old saying that is just as relevant as ever. You should always hope for the very best possible outcome, yet you should always prepare for the very worst possible catastrophe. Whether it is something as serious as a flood, hurricane, earthquake, or tornado, hope that it will not strike you but prepare for it to strike you. Or take, for example, even something as silly as winning the lottery. You can hope to get rich winning the lottery, but you better be prepared to keep working your day job. To hope for the best yet prepare for the worst is a great train of thought.

Maelstrom

If you want to survive, do not put all your eggs in one basket. For instance, what if you have one main customer or one main supplier that you deal with exclusively and then something happens, such as the people that you have been dealing with for years leave, die, get fired, or the company gets bought out. You do not know how the relationship will continue with the new people. It is fine to have one main client as long as losing them would not be enough to sink you.

Synergy

If you are the best at something or somewhat of a perfectionist, then it will be hard for others to perform to your standards. If you need something done right, you can always do it yourself. Except if you do everything yourself, then you limit how much you can produce. In times when production requires you to run a crew, your time is better spent making sure your crew is using the best possible methods and procedures. No matter how good you are, you cannot outwork a crew. Make sure your crew is lined out and working efficiently before going at it yourself.

Production

Consistency and sticking to the basics are good. Day in and day out, use the techniques that are proven. For reliability you should stick with what you know, but you should always try to improve upon and develop new systems and procedures. Trying to improve is important; your competitors do it, but try to experiment when it will not get in the way of performance or production.

Ingenuity

Sometimes it is necessary to conform to standards or to get by with what works, but whenever possible, think of ways to enhance or improve. There is usually always a way to make it better or even just to simplify. Think outside of the box. Sometimes there are ways to make the unthinkable possible, like figuring out a way to fit ten gallons of water into a five-gallon bucket. If there is a will, there is a way.

Check It Twice

Measure twice and cut once, as the old saying goes. It is better to take the time to measure two, even three times in order to get it right. If you measure it once and mistakenly make the measurement wrong, then the piece is cut wrong. Consequently, you will still have to measure a second time, but this time on the new piece. Although the method of double-checking is time-consuming, it can be more efficient in the end.

Clearly the method of double-checking applies to more than just cutting something.

Don't Measure

Whenever possible, do not measure at all. Set up a template, benchmark, grid, or story pole. The fewer times you have to measure or double check, the more you will produce. However, you should triple check the measurement on your pattern and do a test run before starting production.

Disposition

It takes years to build a reputation, yet in the beginning it only takes days to destroy it. It seems, whatever your reputation is, it is exaggerated. If it is for being honest, you were the most honest person they ever knew. If it was for being fair, you were the fairest person they ever knew. If you build a bad reputation, it will be exaggerated in the same way. Try to build on and improve upon your reputation. It is very important.

Forsaken

Be careful what you wish for because you just might get it. This is a hard lesson to learn. It is like wanting a different lover and then you end up with the new lover only to realize that the lover you have forsaken was the better lover, the one who truly loved you, and the one you truly loved. Do not forsake what you have. Learn to love, appreciate, and value it. Sometimes you do not realize what you have until it is gone.

Excessive

If you are high all the time, then being high is no longer a good or fun thing; it is normalcy. Sometimes you must feel bad in order to feel good. Moderation is important with all things.

Without the sun there would be no life on this planet, yet too much sun can cause heat stroke or skin cancer. You need food to survive, yet too much food can make you overweight and lead to obesity and diabetes. You must have an abundance of water to live, yet if you drink too much water too fast, it can kill you. Too much of anything is bad for you.

Self-Control

Self-control is very important. You should practice it. There may come a time when you are trying to quit something, like smoking for example. In order to quit, you have to want to quit. All the medication and clinics in the world cannot help you quit if you do not want to quit. You should do things like tell yourself that dirty ashtrays are disgusting, but do not clean them. Leave them around so you get tired of seeing them. Their smell and their flavor will soon begin to make you sick. When you are not smoking and you smell second-hand smoke, tell yourself the smell is sickening and that smoking is a filthy habit. This will sink into your brain and soon you will want to quit. Once you want to do it, then you will do it.

Walk The Line

We spend our whole lives trying to gain control, whether it is moving away from home, getting our own car, or trying to avoid arrest. Nonetheless, as young adults we discover partying; little do we realize that this haze we enter into takes our control away. We go from being able to think straight and acting right to impairing our own ability to drive. Having a clear mind gives you control.

Clear Mind

When your hand or foot falls asleep, you will try to shake it out so it will feel normal again. Your mind is not unlike any other part of your body. If your mind is numb, that may stop you from feeling the bad feelings, but it also shuts out the good feelings. Why go through life foggy-headed. Try it with a clean and clear mind. You will be able to think better and clearer. You will feel what you are supposed to feel. Walk the straight line.

It is all about what you want to do; if you want to drink, you will drink. If there comes a time you need to stop, then there is only one thing that can make you stop: you. There are not twelve steps to sobriety; there is one step: you.

CHAPTER 6

Conversing

Writing A Letter

In business you must be able to write a powerful letter. Of course, nowadays with computer programs helping you with spelling, grammar, and so on, it is much easier to write a letter. Nevertheless, a letter must be based purely on facts. If you write a letter based on facts, it will be very hard for others to argue it, disagree with it, or oppose it. Whether you are good at writing a letter or not, it must be factual. That is the key to a powerful letter.

Everybody Knows

Sooner or later everybody knows everything. Live every day as though everyone knows everything about you and you may not be caught off guard when somebody tells you something that you thought was privileged information.

You may try to keep competitors from knowing about your business, but eventually they will know everything about it. If you go through life as though everybody knows everything about you, then you will never have to react to their actions. Instead you can focus on the task at hand and move forward accordingly.

Negotiating

In negotiations you must always give people or leave people a way out. Even if you are absolutely right, if you back them into a corner, they will fight you every inch of the way. To get someone to admit that they made a mistake, misunderstood, or just did not communicate correctly is achievable. On the other hand, to get someone to admit to flat out lying, purposely deceiving, or being dead wrong is not an easy thing to accomplish.

Meeting With Others

Before meeting with others, you should first figure out what the best- and worst-case scenarios would be, then what the fairest agreement would be. Then when the time comes to meet, do not be the first one to speak your mind or to show your hand. If possible, let others go first so you may see their side and better know how to play yours. It might be that they start out by offering more than you expected. Consequently, you would not have gotten as much if you would have spoken first.

There is also the tactic of sandbagging. When you have to show your hand, show only what or as much as you have to. Try not to reveal the ace in the hole, so to speak, until it is needed.

Accord

Sometimes you can reach an agreement and sometimes you cannot. When people have their minds set, they may not be able to see things from your point of view. It is important to get your point across but you do not necessarily need to get their agreement. In times when you cannot agree, you can agree to disagree.

Hearing

When someone is talking to you, give them your full attention. Focusing on the immediate moment should be your only task at hand. It is very important to recognize the person who is trying to communicate with you, and you should expect the same consideration in return.

Listening

When an elder is telling a story, even if it is a story you have heard many times before, listen in closely. Although you may have heard it before, you may understand it differently because of where you are in life. If you hear a story when you are a teenager, you may comprehend only so much or only in a certain way. If you hear that same story when you are in your thirties, you may perceive it in a totally different way. Try to understand all that the elder is trying to pass on to you through the story.

Courteous

Always show courtesy to people. When somebody takes the time or goes out of their way to tell you something, whether it is good or bad, you should be thankful. Even when you have to deal with people that you do not like, you should still be courteous.

Naysayer

Believe nothing you hear and only half of what you see. This is a very old saying, but it is only half true nowadays because in this day and age, with computer graphics and picture cropping, it is also hard to believe anything you see. You should keep in mind that when something is taken out of context, even a picture, it could appear as though it is something it is not. Someone else may want you to see something a certain way. Things are not always as they appear.

Your Word

Your word is your bond, but only if you are a man of your word. If you say you are going to do something, then do it. You are only as good as your word; this is what makes a man dignified.

Be cautious. Do no take someone else's word for granted unless they have earned your trust or are trustworthy.

Don't Speak In Anger

It is better not to speak out of anger. You might regret what you say or at least say things that you would not normally say. It is much better if you can give it some time. If your convictions are strong, then you will still feel the same later on, though you will voice yourself much better.

Talk Clearly And Be Decisive

When you speak try to talk as clearly and communicate as decisively as you can. Try not to mumble or stutter; try not to talk in circles or to repeat yourself. Do not ramble on. Get to the point and say what needs to be said.

Say What You Mean

Say what you mean and mean what you say. Do not say something that you do not mean. If you do, take it back at once. If you think there may be some confusion or misunderstanding, then do your best to clarify what you are trying to say. Try to be very explicit when talking.

Straight Shooter

Sometimes the truth hurts, hence the term brutally honest. Tell it like it is and do not hold back even if you are concerned with the reaction you will get. It is better to be honest even if it will anger or sadden the one or others you are telling the truth to. By doing so you will gain the respect of others.

Careful What You Say

Be careful about what you say and where you say it. Sometimes your opponent can tell what you are thinking or what move you are going to make from a simple word, phrase, or even a gesture. This can give your opponent the advantage.

Professing

If you let it be known that you are the best at something, then people will expect you to be the greatest there has ever been. However, if you let it be known that you are just okay at something, then it will be easier to impress. Be careful what you profess.

Don't Talk Too Much

Always be truthful, but do not volunteer information. Do not talk too much. When asked a question, answer it truthfully but do not carry on. Less is more. If it is possible to explain something in ten words instead of thirty words, then do it.

Misgiving

As the old saying goes, you can fool some of the people some of the time but not all of the people all of the time. You may think no one knows when you are exaggerating, but you may only be fooling yourself.

If you catch yourself telling someone something that is not totally true, then immediately correct yourself. If you take it back quickly enough, it will be as if you did not mean it. Honesty is first and foremost.

Discretion

Think before you speak. Sometimes it is better not to say anything at all and let people think you are unintelligent than it is to speak up and prove to everyone that you are unintelligent. Think about what you are going to say and when you are going to say it, or if anything at all needs to be said.

Wisdom

You can tell someone is wise by the way they speak. Maybe someone has only been doing something for one year and after they fix something they are quick to say, "I know it's right." This is not wise. Then someone else who has been doing the same thing for ten years fixes it and says, "I think it's right." This is a wise way to speak. With age comes experience, knowledge, and wisdom, but on occasion people may be wise beyond their years.

All Talk

Talk is cheap. Actions speak louder than words. Whenever possible, show instead of telling. You should keep in mind that if enough people say something is so, then perhaps it is. If enough people vouch for something or rally against something, then this should weigh into your actions but not your opinion. You should not give an opinion on something that you have not experienced but have only heard others talk about. Until you have experienced it for yourself, you cannot voice a true opinion on it.

Hypocritical

As the saying goes, practice what you preach. No one will respect you if you go around telling everyone alcohol is bad for you and then you get caught drinking a margarita. Do not think of telling others to do as you do not. It is very important to do as you say.

Know All

Do not become a know-it-all. You should not be one of those people who will not listen to suggestions, will not take advice, and will not heed warnings. It will hold you back and keep you from improving yourself and your abilities. If you act like you know it all, then eventually the time will come when you are wrong, thus proving your ignorance. You have only begun to learn; suffice it to say, you should never proclaim to know all about anything.

CHAPTER 7

In the End

How Precious Each Moment Of Life Is

This is a quote from Brandon Lee in 1993, just a few days before he died: "Because we do not know when we will die, we get to think of life as an inexhaustible well. And yet everything happens only a certain number of times, a very small number really. How many more times will you remember a certain afternoon of your childhood, an afternoon that is so deeply a part of your being that you cannot even conceive of your life without it, perhaps four or five times more. Perhaps not even that. How many more times will you watch the full moon rise, perhaps twenty and yet it all seems limitless."

The Way Of The Samurai

The state of being a samurai: its basis lies in accepting death and not fearing it, in devoting oneself to one's master and one's trade, in living in each moment and appreciating each moment for what it is worth, in making the most out of each day and each action performed, and in taking pride in oneself and respecting others.

Samurai who lived hundreds of years ago were more honorable than many people of this day and age. Ancient Japan was more civilized than many countries of today. The way of the samurai was and is a good outlook on life.

The Way

The beliefs in this book are some of the things that I have learned along my way. I hope some of them will help you along yours. While some are derived from the way of the samurai, the vast majority came from my father. He taught me more about life than I could ever convey.

The Ending

This too shall pass; whether it is good or bad, everything will eventually end. When you are experiencing pain or are in a bad situation, remember this too shall pass. There is an end to everything. Understanding that the end is important in all things, even life, is train of thought.

Lightning Source UK Ltd.
Milton Keynes UK
18 January 2010

148751UK00001B/192/A